TEACHER

— creating conversational community —

David Francis   Ken Braddy   Michael Kelley

David Francis
Director of Sunday School at LifeWay. Member of the Minister of Education tribe. Preschool Sunday School teacher with wife, Vickie. Dad to 3 sons. Grandaddy to 5. Author of 13 books. 12 are free on iTunes or at *LifeWay.com/ DavidFrancis*.

Ken Braddy
Manager of LifeWay's ongoing Bible studies for adults. Co-author of *3 Roles For Guiding Groups*. Veteran Minister of Education. Blogger on the topics of Sunday School and groups (*KenBraddy.com*). Conference leader and trainer of teachers. Shepherds a new Sunday School group for empty-nesters with wife, Tammy.

Michael Kelley
Director of Groups Ministry at LifeWay. Father of three. Husband of one, Jana. Church elder. Author of *Wednesdays were Pretty Normal, Faith Limps, Holy Vocabulary, Hard Sayings of Jesus,* and *Boring.* Blogger (*MichaelKelleyMinistries.com*).

© 2015 LifeWay Press

Permission is granted to photocopy this resource. Free downloadable versions are available online at *LifeWay.com/DavidFrancis* or the iTunes store.

Additional material not included in the print version is also available for free download at the website listed above, including teaching plans and PowerPoint® presentations that support the book.

ISBN 9781430055099
Item 006104039

By completing a study of this book, you can receive course credit in the Christian Growth Study Plan. For more information, visit *LifeWay.com/CGSP*.

Dewey decimal classification: 268.0
Subject headings: SUNDAY SCHOOLS/RELIGIOUS EDUCATION

Unless otherwise noted, all Scripture quotations are taken from the HCSB, © 1999, 2999, 2002, 2003, 2009 by Holman Bible Publishers. Used by permission.

Printed in the United States of America

Contents

"Teacher" *4*

They called Him Teacher. He calls you to be a teacher. It is a call to create conversational community.

Chapter 1: Conversational Community *5*

Conversational community describes the group experience and the outcome of that experience. Conversational community is seen in the research-validated Transformational Sweet Spot. The four voices of conversational community are the Bible, the Holy Spirit, the Learners, and the Teacher. A lesson planning framework simply called Say/Ask/Do helps the teacher plan for all four voices to be heard.

Chapter 2: Say *24*

What are you going to say? What does the Bible say? How do you use stories skillfully? What about visual aids? The cutting room floor paradox and dump trucks remind us that less is more and lead us to totally reject premastication.

Chapter 3: Ask *35*

Good questions matter. So does silence. We can anticipate questions that may be asked of us. What are you going to do about the member who dominates discussion? Adult teachers could learn from preschool teachers.

Chapter 4: Do *46*

We can do more than just saying and asking. Obedience is the outcome of true conversational community, especially obedience to the Great Commission by sprinkling salt as you go. "Conversation" refers to "walk" as well as "talk."

"Teacher" *58*

Imagine your memorial service. Will they remember you as "teacher"?

Appendix: Creating a Development Plan *59*

A list of topics to include when creating a development plan for those called to teach people the Bible.

Endnotes *62*

Documentation from some really good resources for additional study.

"Teacher"

They called Him Teacher. He liked it.[1] When He had something really important to say, He often sat down. Once He sat in a boat, employing the water as an amplifier. He sat on a hillside to give His longest recorded talk. You can read it out loud in about 18 minutes. Most of the time, conversational volume would do. He was a story teller. A really good one. When He had something really, really important to say, He sat down with a small group of 12. Sometimes they needed to ask what a story meant. He let them. They were a conversational community.

He knew every word of the Bible. Yet He would ask others what they thought it meant. The whole world around Him was a resource room of visual aids and object lessons. Flowers. Birds. Vines. Branches. Bread. Cups. Basins. Towels. Kids. He liked kids. He said those who "get" heaven's kingdom enter it like a kid.

He taught while He walked. He walked a lot. One of His last walks was after a closed group dinner in an upper room. The destination was a garden. It was a night of heart-deep teaching.[2] One follower paid particularly close attention, tagging Him as The Word. Before the sun set the next day, the Word was in a tomb. He walked to His execution, bearing history's most enduring object lesson. With His final breaths, He taught. Paradise. Thirst. Forgiveness. Forsaken. Finished. Mother. Father.

The tomb could not contain the Word. Alive again, He went for a walk. He entered into a conversation with two guys. He taught His disciples. Before giving His final instructions, He taught. He opened their minds to understand the Scriptures. Then, He gave commands for "as you go." Make disciples. Baptize. Teach.

As a teacher, you continue His teaching ministry. You are part of heaven's Special Forces, called to create conversational community.

Chapter 1
Conversational Community

Are you a new teacher? Considering volunteering as a teacher? Already a teacher? Maybe the role is called Sunday School teacher. Maybe LIFE Group leader. Perhaps small group shepherd. Whatever the official name of the program or position, your primary responsibility is to guide a group that gathers—maybe weekly—to discover and apply Bible truth.

For many years now, church leaders have tried to find a better noun to describe those who guide Bible study in groups. But "teacher" endures. Perhaps that's because two popular alternatives—leader and shepherd—are sort of included with teacher; but teacher is not necessarily included with them.

In reality, if people call you "teacher," that's what you are, officially or not. "Teacher" sounds beautiful coming from the mouth of a preschooler, even if they are getting your attention to tattle! How rewarding it is to walk into a hospital room and watch a member's face brighten as she introduces you to her family as "my Sunday School teacher," even if the official title is something else. If you're going to be called a name, "teacher" surpasses most.

> ### Conversational community won't happen without a lead learner called to create it.

Let us be very clear about what we mean by "teacher." We don't mean a Bible expert who stands behind a lectern, talking to a group of people sitting in rows, expecting them to listen with agreement, amazement, and admiration. We understand the comfort many find in that approach. Some risks are minimized and anyone can at least listen. But if that's your vision, this book may actually make you mad. We hope you're open to an idea of "teacher" that means a lead learner "creating conversational community."

Community is not measured as much by closeness as by conversation.

Think about the last time you tried to have a single group conversation in an SUV. Or a 15-passenger van. Or a tour bus. You probably knew the other people in the vehicle. Perhaps well. There was probably some sense of relational community. You at least shared destinational community. But it is unlikely you came close to conversational community.

Sometimes it is better to describe a concept than to define it.

Conversational community is probably one such concept. What do you think when you hear those words? What do you feel? Do you remember being part of a group this term fits? What were the characteristics of the group that made it a conversational community? Did it have a person who was designated as the leader? Did the group look to him or her as the teacher, whether or not he or she officially had that title? What was it about that person that caused members to think of them as teacher? What excites you most about creating this kind of community? What roadblocks must be overcome for you to create this kind of community?

Presentation to people sitting in rows is a great way to disseminate information and sabatoge transformation.

Conversation trumps presentation almost every time as a vehicle for spiritual transformation. Community that accelerates transformation is best done in circles. We believe that groups pursuing and practicing conversational community are the best environment for people to be in a posture to experience the *Transformational Sweet Spot* (TSS).[3]

The Transformational Sweet Spot

A group of people who hear the same thing doesn't always hear the same thing.

Ever play a sport like tennis or baseball with a ball and a stick? If you have, then you know what the "sweet spot" is. It's that place on the bat or racket that, when it strikes the ball, is able to somehow propel it further and faster than other spots on your equipment. It's the singular place where things come together to produce maximum impact.

There's a sweet spot in discipleship, and like in these sports, it's the place where three things converge together. In a sentence, the transformational sweet spot is the intersection of truth given by healthy leaders when someone is in a vulnerable posture.

Godly leaders. Biblical truth. Humble posture. When those three things happen in the same place at the same time, transformation is likely to occur. But think about how easily that environment can be corrupted if one of those factors is missing.

For example, you might have a group of people hungry for the truth. You might even have a well-intentioned leader. But unless the centerpiece of the conversation in that environment is the living and active Word of God, you might have a great discussion, but nobody's going to walk away transformed by the power of the Holy Spirit.

Similarly, you might have a willing and godly leader. That leader might be presenting biblical truth in a group. But unless the people in that group are in a humble and teachable posture, then it will be like a farmer sowing seeds on ground hardened by the sun.

Sound familiar? It's that last example that points us back to the necessity of conversational community. When a person is allowed to simply sit and soak, they are far more likely to have a posture of hardness to truth.

But when we move people out of the comfortable silence and solitude of rows and into circles, suddenly there is an expectation of participation. A group in which people participate is much more likely to be a group receptive to the convicting and transformative power of the Holy Spirit.

Not only that, but a conversational and participatory environment like this provides a greater opportunity for people to see God's truth applied specifically to a situation in their own life through the voice and experience of someone else.

In environments like this, the Holy Spirit uses not only the leader but also individual group members to speak to each other. Through sharing their experiences, their struggles, and their stories of God's faithfulness, they spur one another on to good deeds and godliness.

As we share with each other like this, we are encouraged to believe that it might actually be true that God cares about the everyday decisions and issues we are facing. It might actually be true that we can make choices that impact the world for Him. It might actually be true that we can walk out of a group, challenged and encouraged, not just to think more but to continue to carry our personal experience into the world around us.

In other words, we might actually embrace the call of Jesus to be salt and light in the world.

In conversational community, we can fill our salt shakers for conversation in our larger community.

Let your conversation be seasoned with salt, that is, with winsomeness, so that you may know how to make a fitting answer to everyone. (Col. 4:6, Williams)[4]

Where do we get salt for everyday conversations? How about in your Bible study group? Think how it would change your approach to group Bible study if a primary goal was for everyone to take some "salt" away from every group experience. A timeless truth, a memorable story, a funny illustration, an interesting fact, a really cool word meaning, a powerful proverb, a beautiful poem, a captivating statement, a convicting command.

Grains of salt you could gently sprinkle into conversations. If that became the goal, it would change not only the way you taught the group; it would also change the way you prepare for it.

The teacher faces two big challenges in order to prepare in this way, both of which are pretty obvious when you think about it.

The first obstacle is about knowledge. Not knowledge of the Bible, but knowledge of the people in your group. When all you do is lecture, the sum total of your relationships with your group members amounts to a handshake and small talk for a few minutes at the beginning. If that's the depth of community in your group, how can you possibly hope to know your people well enough to craft an illustration, presentation, or question that would communicate most effectively to them so they might walk away challenged to live differently?

The second obstacle is about humility. In order to have this kind of conversational community, we as leaders and teachers must be humble enough to share the authority and platform God has given us. We must be willing to let others talk, to ask them what they think, and then to actually listen. By sharing the platform, you put the group in a better position for the Holy Spirit to communicate, convict, and challenge.

Both of these obstacles have their source in our pride. One of the main reasons some shy away from this kind of a conversational environment is because down deep in our hearts we want to be the great expert. We want to be the mouthpiece. We want to have the spotlight. If we search our hearts and find this kind of latent pride lurking there, then we must also recognize that it's not only sinful, it's illogical. There are ideally multiple voices in a conversational community.

If you listen, you'll hear four voices in conversational community.

Recently, I (David) met retired Minister of Education Maurice Hodges. Still passionate about training teachers, Maurice sent me a copy of a training plan he developed three decades ago. The concepts and principles he included are remarkably timeless and are best experienced in a conversational community. His course "Bible Teaching to Change Lives" included four sessions built around the four voices present in a Sunday School class:[5]

The Bible	The Holy Spirit
The subject, study helps, interpretation	Conviction, conversion, spiritual growth
The Teacher	The Learners*
Bible study, lesson plans, dynamic session	Needs, interests, experiences, problems

*Hodges used "Pupil." We will often use "learners" or "group members" as an equivalent term.

These terms point to the four "voices" in a conversational community. They are woven into the fabric of this book. Our basic premise is that an essential task of every teacher is to make a thorough study of the Bible passage the group will explore, and then determine what they will say, what they will ask, and what the group will do.

The plan will be even more effective if it is developed with the learners clearly in mind.

It will be more transformational still if it is undergirded by a desperate dependence on the Holy Spirit.

Finally, the group experience will produce greater learning the more it feels like a conversation, not just a presentation. That, we believe, is a simple formula to guide learning.

The Bible is central to this entire process. It, too, has a voice. The most important voice, in fact.

The Bible

The essential voice in conversational community is the Bible.

Studying and teaching the Bible is different than studying and teaching based on any other source. The Bible is the Word of God. It is the living revelation of the living God. It is God's Story. No one's story is complete until it has intersected with God's Story.

A key document that guides the development of Bible study materials created by LifeWay is *The Baptist Faith & Message*. With regard to the Bible, it states:

> *The Holy Bible was written by men divinely inspired and is God's revelation of Himself to man. It is a perfect treasure of divine instruction. It has God for its author, salvation for its end, and truth, without any mixture of error, for its matter. Therefore, all Scripture is totally true and trustworthy. It reveals the principles by which God judges us, and therefore is, and will remain to the end of the world, the true center of Christian union, and the supreme standard by which all human conduct, creeds, and religious opinions should be tried. All Scripture is a testimony to Christ, who is Himself the focus of divine revelation.* [6]

"Bible" is one of ten key spiritual concepts for kids identified in the Levels of Biblical Learning.[7] This document guides the creation of Bible studies for kids by LifeWay. The concepts are:

God	Jesus	Holy Spirit
Bible	Salvation	Creation
Church	People	Family
Community/World		

In the Levels of Biblical Learning document, each of these concepts is further defined in developmental terms. Here's what kids can master about the concept "Bible" as they develop from infants to preteens. As you review these, notice the progression.

Younger Preschoolers	**The Bible is a special Book.** The Bible tells about God. People in the Bible told about God. The Bible tells about Jesus. The Bible helps me know what to do.
Middle Preschoolers	**The stories in the Bible really happened.** The Bible teaches us what God is like. People in the Bible wrote about God. The Bible teaches what Jesus did. The Bible teaches right from wrong.
Older Preschoolers	**Everything in the Bible is true.** The Bible teaches us what God and Jesus are like. People wrote God's words in the Bible. The Bible teaches that Jesus died on a cross. The Bible teaches right and wrong.
Younger Kids	**Bible truths never change.** The Bible helps me know more about God, Jesus, and the Holy Spirit. God helped people know what to write in the Bible. The Bible teaches that Jesus died on a cross, was buried, and was raised from the dead. The Bible teaches how God wants me to live.
Middle Kids	**The truths in the Bible will last forever.** The Bible is God's message about Himself. God inspired people to know what to write in the Bible. The Bible teaches that Jesus died on a cross, was buried, and was raised from the dead. The Bible teaches how to live the Christian life.
Preteens	**The truths in the Bible are without error and will last forever.** The Bible is God's message about Himself and His plan for salvation. The Bible is the only inspired, written Word of God. The Bible teaches that salvation through Jesus is God's gift of salvation. The Bible teaches how to live a Christian life by following Jesus.

The Bible is central to this idea of conversational community. It doesn't matter what we say until we are clear about what the Bible has to say. That is the beginning of preparing to teach.

Every curriculum we are personally involved with not only provides teaching tools like a Leader Guide, but also provides several other resources to help equip the teacher to find clarity in their own minds about the message of Scripture.

Using these tools, a teacher can dig into the greater context of a passage of Scripture. This is an imperative part of the preparation process because every single text was originally written to a specific group of people at a specific time for a specific occasion. Until we understand the historical context, we can't rightly help people understand what the text truly says.

Furthermore, every text is set inside of a larger text, a book of the Bible. And each book is set inside a specific genre of literature. Understanding these genres of Scripture further informs our interpretation of what individual passages mean.

Still further, every book of the Bible is found within the overall story of the whole Bible. We must understand the thrust of the entire story in order to see where its individual parts reside.

The Bible can't say what it never said.

Imagine for a second picking up a piece of correspondence. You might read names, dates, and mentions of specific things. But until you know who wrote the letter, why they wrote it, who they wrote it to, and even some of what was happening in the world at that time, you don't really understand the letter you hold.

This takes a little work. Important work. We should have a holy pause every time we consider the gravity of what we are dealing with when we stand or sit with a group of people with Bibles in hand. There are no greater issues in the universe than what we will be discussing.

But God has not left us to do this work alone. There are leader guides, commentaries, dictionaries, systematic theologies, and a host of other resources we can use to aid our study. But the greatest asset God has given us is the Holy Spirit. He is our trustworthy Guide in preparing to teach.

The Holy Spirit

You are not the only teacher in the room.

Jesus told His disciples that the Holy Spirit would guide them into the truth (see John 16:13). When you and I stand in front of a group as teacher, the Teacher stands with us. The Holy Spirit invites us to be His partner in this process we call group Bible study.

One unfortunate philosophy of teaching Scripture involves what you could call the "fall open" method. It's basically the idea that we can stand in front of a group of people, open up the Word of God at random, and then trust the Holy Spirit to communicate something through us or in spite of us.

That's certainly not out of the realm of possibility; most every teacher has had the experience in the middle of leading a group when they sensed the Holy Spirit taking the conversation in a different direction. We should be ready and able to adapt to the blowing winds of the Holy Spirit in a given moment. But trusting in the Holy Spirit is not a substitute for preparation.

The Holy Spirit is not bound to move and work only within a gathered group. He can guide you in preparation as much as He can guide you during the actual group time. As partners with the Holy Spirit, we must spend time planning out what we as a team will do. Good partners plan.

We honor the Lord by taking the time to prepare well. Furthermore, if we have done that preparation, we will be more sensitive to the ebb and flow at that moment wherever the Holy Spirit might lead.

The Learners

If you teach only how you like to learn, those who learn differently may not get what you teach.

After a teacher has considered the biblical text, attention should be given to the needs of the members. Some developmental needs are shared across an age group or life stage. Others are specific to individuals. What in their lives is addressed by this lesson? What painful memories might this passage bring to the surface? What relationship issues might it confront? What social or political rabbits might it tempt a group member to chase?

Since you default to your preferred learning style, using the other seven must be intentional.

Howard Gardner of Harvard University identified what he called seven "intelligences." His theory emerged from cognitive research and helps us understand the differences in people's minds and how they process information, which affects understanding.[8] Following Thomas Armstrong, LifeWay expanded the list from seven intelligences or learning styles to eight, adding "Natural" to the list.[9]

Which of the eight learning approaches is your "go to" when you teach? It is highly likely that this is the way you prefer to learn. So you teach that way, too. The chart that follows provides a short description of the type of learner represented by each of the eight learning approaches. You'll find a list of activities they prefer. There will be people in your group who enjoy one or more of these approaches, but you can be assured that all eight will be liked by someone. God designed everyone to learn in a different way.

You might refer back to this page after you've read "Chapter 4: Do." The point is to strive to communicate God's Word to people who have different learning preferences.

(Caution: Never try to use all eight in any one session!)

	Learning Approaches	Teaching Methods
Relational	Highly social, make friends easily, may be very good talkers, "people-persons."	*case study, small groups, personal sharing, testimony, storytelling, debate, interview, discussion, biblical simulation, dialogue, role play, skit, games, brainstorming, problem solving that depends on others*
Verbal	Learn best through words—reading, writing, speaking, listening, like the sounds of words	*lecture, question/answer, brainstorming, case study, resource persons, listening teams, personal sharing, oral reading, debate, interview, writing words for songs, monologue, dialogue, paraphrase Scripture, storytelling, panel, skit, games*
Visual	"Create their own pictures" and visuals of what they are learning, "see" in their imaginations if no concrete visuals	*videos, movie clips, posters, charts, maps, object lessons, asking "what if" questions, watching drama, collage, drawing diagrams, wire or paper sculpture*
Reflective	Understand who they are and how they feel, comfortable with periods of quiet	*lecture, case study, question/answer, open-ended sentences, attitude scale, creative writing, diary or journal, listening guides, worksheets and study guides, written tests, listening to music, opinionnaire*
Logical	Enjoy problem solving, reason through difficult situations, rely on analogies	*written test, lecture, worksheets or study guides, notebook, outline, word study, statistics, debate, panel, questions that help discern relationships*
Physical	Very active, have good coordination, play out a story, enjoy "hands-on" activities	*Move to agree/disagree poster, join hands in a circle, art activities (wire/paper sculpture, paper tearing, painting, etc.), arranging room, games, singing with motions, biblical simulation, skit, role play*
Musical	Enjoy music, tend to be good listeners, easy to express themselves through music	*write words for well-known hymns, records, CDs, find hymns relating to the lesson, comparing words of hymns to Scripture, listening to recorded music (sacred or secular)*
Natural	Enjoy the beauty, investigation and exploration of God's creation	*collect or display items from nature, nature walk, sort items from nature, classify items from nature, observe natural items, protect God's world, plant and cultivate, reflect on or relate to creation and the Creator*

If all you expect members to do is show up,
all they will do is show up.

If we care about discipleship, shouldn't we expect more from people than just their attendance? While the list of learning approaches suggests that people want to do something more than just show up, they will settle for doing what is expected of them. Group members should be expected to make preparation for discussion in their Bible study group. The easiest way to express that expectation is to provide everyone with a Personal Study Guide. There is virtually no debate that when members, even if it is only some part of them, show up having done some level of preparation, the conversation will be increasingly more meaningful.

Discipleship should happen whether the member
shows up for the group or not.

Where did we get the idea that people can only learn in a group? Certainly not from research. To be sure, research on measurable year-over-year spiritual growth shows clearly that church attendance and participation in a small group are key factors in such demonstrated growth. But they are the second and third most important factors. The most important—even more than the two factors above—is regular reading of the Bible and other Christian literature.[10] Shouldn't we expect members to "keep up" with the group study—whether or not they are in attendance every time?

It's not about Personal Study Guides.
It's about discipleship.

All three of us make a living selling curriculum materials, and each of us can be as cynical (questioning motives) and skeptical (questioning "facts") as anyone we know. So we've examined our hearts on this. In answer to our inner skeptics, we've seen the research—in great detail. It does matter whether people read biblical materials. It matters a lot. In answer to the cynic in each of us, we really do care about helping the church in her mission of making disciples—whatever publisher is trusted for curriculum. We have some concerns. We think they deserve discussion.

We are troubled by several practices in churches that make the challenge of making disciples more difficult:

- *Groups are meeting less frequently.*
- *Even "active" members are attending less frequently.*
- *Attendance is the only expectation of most members.*
- *Members are not provided Bible study materials of their own.*
- *Thus, they have no materials to study when they miss the group time.*
- *Therefore, discipleship is dependent on unprepared members with less-than-perfect attendance in groups that typically meet less frequently than they once did.*

So, we really believe that it is more crucial than ever in today's changing environment that we:

- *Focus on the key indicator of spiritual growth: "self-feeding" on the Bible and other biblical material.*
- *Provide Bible study material that is part of a "map" for discipleship.*
- *Expect members to use the materials to prepare for group conversation, whether they are present or not.*
- *Equip parents to have conversations with their kids about their Bible study group experience.*

Personal Study Guides (PSGs) and Kids Activity Pages are part of a wise plan and are relatively inexpensive solutions. But it's really about discipleship. Some groups don't meet every week. Some members don't attend every week. But...

Discipleship should never take a week off.

We asked Shelly Taylor, who directs the preschool and children's ministry at First Baptist Church, Dallas, Texas, what they do to partner with parents in the spiritual growth of their kids. Here is what we learned:

*We do multiple things to assist parents in preparing their children for Sunday School and reinforcing what they learn. It begins with our ministry to expectant couples. We host **Dinner and Decaf** twice a year. After dinner, I share the heart of our ministry in building a trust relationship with* *parents. We talk about our protective policies and procedures. We share how teaching begins in the baby room. I share how this builds from our youngest room all the way through our 6th grade classes (using Biblical Levels of Learning). It is always exciting to see their eyes light up when they realize their baby is learning in the first room.*

*Each **Thursday** afternoon I send an email to all parents and prospects about the Bible content we will be teaching on Sunday. We encourage parents to introduce this truth first at home. On **Sunday morning**, this truth is introduced at the **classroom door** to the child and parent as they drop off. Example: "Today, we are going to be learning about how Jesus read the Scroll at church." This truth is printed on labels and placed on all activities the child takes home.*

*As parents pick up children, teachers share one thing the child did in the classroom as they were learning that one truth. We also **send home the Take-Home Page** to reinforce what we taught.*

*For children who are not in attendance, we mail the Take-Home Page with a note letting them know what we learned. I almost stopped due to expense, but that very week I heard from people who had been receiving them. One came to Sunday School after being out for months. They had gone through a very difficult time financially and could not afford the gas to drive to downtown. The mom tearfully expressed her thankfulness and how she used them to teach her children the lessons they were missing. Another family shared that they came back to church because they realized how much instruction their children were missing. Another family shared that they were using the pages as the basis for their family devotion. So we still **mail the Take-Home Pages to absentees.***

*Sunday School teachers are also encouraged to **call their children** and let them know what they will be learning on Sunday and share something exciting they will be doing that coming week. It's really just the work of the Sunday School and prayers of His people as we do everything we can think of to connect with our families through multiple touch points.*[11]

Thanks, Shelly. We can't improve on that!

Taking Cookies to a Neighbor

Take-Home Activity Pages are primarily for the parents. Will's mom was so glad to retrieve his Activity Page. She had been looking for a way to meet their new neighbors and invite them to church. One of the ideas on the Activity Page included baking cookies with your child and delivering the cookies to a neighbor. Will helped his mom in the kitchen as they talked about what it means to be a good neighbor. When they delivered the cookies, Will got to tell their neighbors all about his Bible study class and why he was delivering the cookies.

Home should be a conversational community, both by itself and as an extension of the conversational communities enjoyed by parents, students, and kids through church. The Activity Pages many churches provide are a perfect catalyst for parents to have a spiritual conversation with their kid(s) about the Bible story or passage explored by their children.

Parents, not teachers, bear the primary responsibility for making disciples of their kids. I love the fact that absentees at FBC Dallas receive copies in the mail. That's quite an investment. Yet it is very consistent with the conviction that discipleship should never take a week off.

Learners learn best from teachers who see themselves as lead learners.

Now Ezra had determined in his heart to study the law of the Lord, to obey it, and to teach its statutes and ordinances in Israel. (Ezra 7:10)

Ezra was a studious and obedient leader who taught truth. Do you know the story? Why were the people in a vulnerable posture to receive truth from a leader? How does this story reflect the three factors that converge at the Transformational Sweet Spot?

Nehemiah 8 names thirteen people who helped smaller groups of people understand the Scripture read to them by Ezra. They had prepared alongside Ezra so they could clarify and explain key ideas. These thirteen "lead learners" were the teachers.

The Teacher

Who we are trumps what, when, how, and even why we teach.

The teacher is the most important lesson. Allan Taylor says that the character needed by a teacher can be summarized with three H's: holy, humble, and hungry.[12] The mark of the teacher is love. Love for each of the three H's above. Love for the Bible. Love for its Hero. Love for the Spirit He sent. Love for the learners. Love for their stories. Love for how those stories weave together into a tapestry of conversational community. Love for how God impacts those stories—individually and collectively—with His Story. Love for a community. Committed to making sure it is a safe place for the longtime attender whose story is well-known and a hospitable place for the newcomer whose story is yet to be heard.

When asked to describe their teacher in one word, the best response is "love."

We measure spiritual maturity in all kinds of ways. We talk about spiritual disciplines, consistency of church attendance, willingness to serve, and even financial stewardship. No doubt all of these things are important, and all are valid markers of maturity in the life of the disciple. But it should matter greatly to us that the defining mark of Jesus' followers, according to Jesus Himself, was love:

> *By this all people will know that you are My disciples, if you have love for one another (John 13:35).*

What we know is important. How we prepare is important. The environment we create is important. But all of them pale in comparison to the way we love.

In the midst of the preparation, we must regularly ask God to renew our love for each other, for Him, and for His Word. We never want to find ourselves among those who can recite information but care little for those seeking transformation.

When you want to know how, simple tools help.

The simple tool we will introduce to help you prepare to lead a group time is a framework built on Say/Ask/Do. When we create a group plan to lead a class or group to discover and apply the truths of the Scripture, we must consider:

- *What will I* **SAY?**
- *What will I* **ASK?**
- *What will we* **DO?**

This basic framework is effective in all environments. All occasions. All locations. It works with all experience levels—including new teachers who have none. It works with all age groups. With kids, it will be reversed: Do/Ssk/Say. The key point of this framework is that there is a lot more to teaching than just the words spoken by the teacher. The stuff that goes on the Say list needs to be culled carefully to make room for the Ask and Do activities that are more likely to create conversational community.

Park on any of these methods for very long and you will lose two-thirds of your group.

Which do groups prefer? Say, Ask, or Do? Rick Yount says that about a third of group members prefer saying. That is, they prefer to listen to a teacher say things. A third prefer asking. They like discussing their teacher's questions. Another third prefer doing. They like hands-on activities that help them learn.[13]

Balance is the key.

Teachers tend to teach in the way they prefer to learn. If teachers primarily use just one way to communicate God's Word, two-thirds of the group members will not engage in learning to the degree they could. Boredom will set in.

Kids almost never prefer sitting and listening. A general rule of thumb is that kids have a hard time paying attention and staying engaged in a learning activity that is longer in minutes than their age in years.

Bible study groups would benefit by having teachers who know how to change things up. But not just for the sake of change. By taking into account how people prefer to learn (and admitting to ourselves that every class or group has all kinds of learners: some who prefer saying, some who prefer asking, and some who prefer doing), we avoid being "gimmicky" in our teaching. We are instead being servants to our group members and meeting their needs.

If you prefer to Say, might you include a few good questions? If you prefer to Ask, might you find a few really interesting things to say or do? If you lean toward Do, like a lot of kids' teachers, do you make adequate preparation to tell the kids the connection between their activities and the lesson or story? We would just exhort you toward balance. We hope the rest of this book will help you.

Some say you can accelerate this planning process by using sound curriculum that employs it.

They are right! Vickie and I (David) teach 4-5 year olds in Sunday School. We can use the process when we need to. Except we would reverse it to Do/Ask/Say. But most Sundays, we don't need to. We just use curriculum materials that incorporate every principle you've read so far.

The pages that follow provide a good way to evaluate curriculum materials—whoever publishes them. Whatever materials you use, think about how they stack up against what you read. If you choose your own passage and procedures each week, your group time will be so much better when you apply the principles of Say/Ask/Do.

Chapter 2
Say

If learning is more than listening, then teaching is more than talking.

Bible preaching and teaching are the primary vehicles for spiritual growth. Jesus employed both. The primary purpose of this book is to help new and veteran teachers engage the groups they lead in conversational Bible study that equips members to become more like Jesus and to share Him with others.

While talking alone is not the same as teaching, nor is listening the same as learning, the spoken word is necessary for both. Teachers say stuff. That's who they are. Members say stuff. That's just natural. Parents say stuff to their kids. That's a command.

Besides, the primary application of every lesson in a conversational community is the "salt" the group will use in their daily conversations. Conversations require talking. Clear, precise, engaging talk stimulates learning—unless only one or two people are doing all the talking.

The best way to figure out what you need to say is to discover what the Word has to say.

Each of us uses a different method to get a handle on the truths of a Bible passage. One approach is not better than the other.

We hope you will find a new idea, or perhaps an affirmation of what you're already doing, as you do what Ezra did: study the Word, obey the Word, and teach the Word to others.

David likes to see the broader context, break the passage into bite-sized chunks, then pull it back together under one big idea.

I (David) have a whole file cabinet filled with folders for each book of the Bible, with notes accumulated over the years using this simple approach. Basically, I type out the passage in little chunks in my base translation down the left side of the page. Then I compare other translations, capture footnotes, study Bible notes, commentary from the Leader Guide and other sources, and illustrations. These are handwritten. Here is a short example using one verse.

1 Cor	Messed up church in city of Corinth, west of Athens. Paul wrote letter after hearing of problems after he departed following 18 months teaching them.		
12:	One problem concerned spiritual gifts. Paul addressed that problem in ch 12-14. Members were bragging "my gift is better than yours."		
	CSB	Compare translations	Notes/Ideas
7	A demonstration of the Spirit is given to each person to produce what is beneficial:	NIV/NAS=the manifestation NIV/NAS=for the common good KJV=to profit withal NLT=so we can help each other	God puts Himself on display when we exercise the gifts He has given us. Greek=s*ympheron* Symphony! Handel's *Messiah*. Teamwork: touchdown vs. a goal line stand. Who scored?
Big idea	God shows Himself in each of us for the purpose of helping all of us. Community!		

Can you see how starting with what the Bible has to say might help you figure out what you will say? Or ask? Or guide the class to do? In this verse, we discover the wonderful gift of the Greek word from which we get the English word "symphony." What a perfect example of teamwork using individual gifts that point to God. That made me think of standing at the end of Handel's Messiah because I am overwhelmed with awe toward Messiah Jesus! Being a football fan, it made me think of a situation and question: End of long drive. Fourth and goal. Time expiring. Running back blasts into the end zone. Who scored the touchdown?

You can imagine how much stuff you could have if there were several verses. Deciding what not to say is as important for a teacher as deciding what to say. So the hard part is going back and putting a big X through a lot of cool stuff I discovered!

The background study is never wasted. Even the stuff I X'd out. In fact, one who teaches more by discussion than lecture will actually need to go deeper than one who only lectures. What?! Yep, it's true. When you control the teaching, or if you are a "save your questions to the end" type of teacher, you get to control the content. If others can ask questions too, a lot more preparation is required. My approach is similar to what Gary Newton calls an "analytical outline."[14] He has refined this approach, giving greater details in his book *Heart-Deep Teaching*.

Ken starts early and studies inductively.

I (Ken) served two great churches as Education Pastor. Both churches were committed to developing strong Sunday Schools with well-equipped and well-trained teachers. One of my bedrock commitments was to help group leaders prepare to teach. We started early in the week. Teacher training was held weekly on Sunday afternoons. Why on Sundays? Two reasons. First, the teaching session from that morning was still fresh on the minds of teachers. They knew what things went well and what needed to be improved. It was a good time to evaluate their teaching ministry. Second, starting our study and preparation early maximized what the Holy Spirit could do with it during the week. We were on the alert for teaching illustrations. We connected real-life events to the Scriptures we taught. It provided us more time to meditate on God's Word. Plus, we did not feel rushed and could take time to consult other study tools such as commentaries, articles, and Leader Guides.

As a lay teacher of a group in my church today, I still have the same personal practice. Before Sunday afternoon is over, I look ahead to the next lesson, read the Bible passage, and begin to let it soak into my heart and mind. Starting early maximizes the Bible study.

Besides starting early, I like taking an inductive approach to Bible study. This follows the pattern of R-O-I-A.

- **Read**. *I read the text over and over for a couple of days.*

- **Observe**. *I jot down words or phrases I don't know or have questions about. I do word studies and research.*

- **Interpret**. *I discover what the text meant to its original audience. I want to make sure I understand the context of the verse, which always has a larger context within the surrounding verses, within the chapter, within the Bible book, and within the Bible as a whole.*

- **Apply**. *I look for ways that I and my group members might live out the biblical text in our particular setting. Is there a command to obey? A sin to avoid? A warning to heed? If I don't connect the text to application, I feel like I've let my group down. I want them leaving our Bible study saying, "I know what I must do this week to live more like Jesus."*

Michael creates a "3 A.M. Statement" and then works backward from there.

I (Michael) have been crafting "3 A.M. Statements" for years, and doing so has been the single most helpful tool of preparation for me in order to teach or preach in any environment. A "3 A.M. Statement" is essentially the main point of what you are trying to get across to the learner.

The reason it's called a "3 A.M. Statement" is because it's a short, memorable phrase that summarizes what your message is about. It's so succinct, if someone called you at 3 A.M. the night before you were teaching and asked what tomorrow's lesson was about, you could quote it to them through the early-morning fog. There are a lot of advantages to teaching this way. Here are two:

1. It isolates the core truth of the message. Many times, I know I walk away from my preparation with lots of great content, so much so that I struggle to remember all the things I want to. But with the "3 A.M. Statement" in my mind, it helps me organize my thoughts and fix on the core of what the Lord said to me.

2. It safeguards the environment. You don't chase rabbits when you have a "3 A.M. Statement." As a teacher (or preacher), the "3 A.M. Statement" serves as a gate for your lesson. In your personal study, you're going to find a ton of information. But with every piece of information, you have to stack it up against your "3 A.M. Statement." It may be really interesting that there are nineteen Greek words for "the" in this passage, but does that fact support the "3 A.M. Statement"? If not, tuck it away for a future time!

Now some people might ask, "Didn't Paul or Jesus or Moses talk about more than one point in a passage?" That depends on how you divide the text. Those guys (Paul, Jesus, Moses) were smart. And they were really, really good communicators. They were thoughtful about their presentations, too. And they were organized. If we take time on the front end to dissect the text appropriately, we get closer to the single thing they were trying to say as they wrote that sentence, paragraph, or paragraphs.

What is not seen and not said is as important to learning as what is seen and said.

Even with minimal preparation, you will have a ton of stuff to answer the question "What are you going to say?" The more difficult but necessary question is: "What aren't you going to say?" As teachers of God's Word, our study and preparation time is a blessing in itself. We learn new things. We discover new insights as the Holy Spirit guides our learning. The big temptation is to act like a "dump truck" and tell the group everything we learned as we studied. Teachers just hate leaving anything out. But we must or risk our brilliance becoming boring. We call this **the cutting room floor paradox.**

Here's our advice. Don't feel like you must tell everything you've discovered. Don't believe you have to use every suggestion in your Leader Guide.

When a movie is produced, lots of good scenes are deleted and left on what is known as "the cutting room floor." This is done so the movie can be shown in the allotted time. You and I, the moviegoers, rarely know what scenes were cut out. We just know that we experienced a great movie.

In a similar manner, the people in your Bible study group won't know exactly what you've left unsaid. Instead of going for the "dump- truck" method of teaching, try approaching the task of teaching like you're cooking using a crockpot. Take it slowly. Let things simmer. Have a long-term view of the teaching-learning process. Save some things to say for another time. Make a note to cover something from the background of the passage at a later date. Be laser-focused as you lead your group. Don't feel like you have to get it all in or else you've cheated your group members. You haven't. Less is more. It's counterintuitive, but true.

Try the dump-truck approach with preschoolers and you'll find them looking for a toy dump truck.

I (David) was responsible for telling the Bible story in our pre-K class. A pretty simple story: Hannah prayed; Samuel was born; He was presented to Eli as vowed; a new robe every year; the end. While preparing, I read several chapters of 1 Samuel to get the background to tell the story well.... in five minutes. With kids, you can keep their attention no longer in minutes than their age in years. By the way, that tops out at 18. Most of the stuff in the first few chapters of 1 Samuel you don't want to tell a preschooler anyway. I left out 95%—at least. But you will cheat them— and yourself—if you just tell the condensed story without understanding the broader context—the stuff you're purposely not going to say. This principle applies to all teachers regardless of the age group they teach.

Premastication may be a yummy way to teach, but it is a yucky way to learn.

Premastication is not some ancient theological term waiting to be rediscovered. It is the practice in the animal kingdom—including some humans who have not discovered the baby food aisle or don't have one—to chew the food intended for their babies. The standard delivery system is to spit the partially digested food into the baby's mouth. Yuck, you say? Well, that's exactly how a lot of teachers feed their classes and groups. The experience of learning a lot of cool stuff by feeding on God's Word is pretty yummy to them. It's pretty yucky if you are on the recipients' end. Especially a dump truck full. We hope you are so grossed out by this idea that you will determine to feed your class in such a way that they have to chew on the Bread of life. OK. Yuck! Let's talk about stories.

When we tell stories well, we are cooperating with how God wired the human brain.

Stories. It's how God wired our brains. He likes stories so much He wrote one! We call it the Bible. It's made up of hundreds of stories. But they are ultimately just part of One Story. It's a story of redemption. Its hero is the Word. The Word who thought up the world and spoke it into being. The Word who spoke to the key characters in the Old Testament. The Word who inspired the wisdom literature in the middle of our Bibles. The Word who spoke through the prophets. The Word who went silent for 400 years then broke the silence by becoming an infant in a feed trough. The Word who visited our planet in the flesh as Jesus of Nazareth. The Word who spoke with an authority never heard before or since. The Word who loved to teach with stories.

Stories were crucial to the teaching ministries of Jesus and Paul. The Lord taught in parables (short stories that were memorable and focused on a single truth). Paul was excellent at creating word pictures using illustrations from everyday life, such as boxing, running, farming, soldiering, and more.

As a teacher, look for stories to share from your own life. Group leaders should practice a level of vulnerability. The people in the group need to see that you don't have it all together. A good teacher will also know his or her group members well enough to call on them to share their own stories. Stories can be powerful tools the Lord uses to shape hearts and open minds.

Illustrations must connect with the audience to be effective. Teachers sometimes make the mistake of going to obscure places in history to make a point. Very few people care what Baron Von-So-and-So did in the twelfth century. Stick with stories that are "closer to home," stories people can relate to. That's another reason to start planning early. You will be more sensitive to stories that relate to the next Bible study session.

In the book *Creative Bible Teaching,* Lawrence Richards and Richard Bredfeldt offer some great advice about the use of stories:

- *Don't tell a story without practice.*

- *Don't make it a sermon.*

- *Keep it vivid. Use words that paint mental pictures.*

- *Avoid too many details.*

- *Resist asking for feedback. Let the story simmer in your listeners' minds.*[15]

The last chapter of your story is not written yet.

One of the marks of a conversational community is that members share their stories, too. The overarching theme of the stories Jesus told, of the illustrations and stories teachers share today, and of the accounts of "overcoming" shared by group members should be that in Christ nobody's story is done as long as they are drawing breath. The stories behind many of the people listed in the lineage of Jesus in Matthew 1 are overwhelming evidence that the story is not over until it's over!

In conversational community, the story is not even over when life is over.

The goal of conversational community is providing salt that gets sprinkled into everyday conversations. Those conversations impact other people's stories. Our kid's stories. Our friend's stories. The stories of people we'll meet only once "as we go."

The end of our story doesn't have to be the end of our story! So make your stories memorable. Brief. Vivid. Stories that can be sprinkled in "salty conversations."

Saying is multiplied by seeing.

"America the Beautiful" paints a word picture, but every word has multiplied impact when accompanied by images of spacious skies, amber waves, purple mountains, fruited plains, and gleaming alabaster cities.

Imagine singing the "Star-Spangled Banner" at its birthplace, Fort McHenry. Fireworks explode perfectly in sync with "the rockets' red glare...the bombs bursting in air." Fighter jets roar overhead just as you sing "the land of the free and the home of the brave." Seeing matters.

By the way, do you know who chaired the convention of the American Sunday School Union in 1834? As a result of that meeting, they launched the Mississippi Valley Enterprise, a monumental effort that planted 5,000 Sunday Schools in America's "western" frontier. Francis Scott Key![16]

Teaching pictures are a tried and true standard.

One of the main tools used by frontier Sunday School missionaries was a "Sunday School paper." We'd call it an Activity Page or Take-Home Sheet today. It featured a Bible story and an illustration. We call that a "teaching picture." Teaching pictures are pretty much standard equipment for teaching kids. The kids in our pre-K class love the oversized poster version we put on the focal wall each week. A smaller version of the same picture is featured at one of the activity centers. Our curriculum comes with a video we use at the end of each session. It shows the same picture as well. And, of course, the Activity Page the kids take home has a small version of the picture along with the Bible story, giving parents a tool for initiating a conversation with their child. Have you heard of the new uptick in coloring books—for adults? Maybe adults would like teaching pictures, too. The visual learners would for sure.

Sometimes people need to engage their physical eyes to illuminate their spiritual eyes.

Your goal is to help people understand, obey, and apply the Word of God. They must see with their spiritual eyes, but that is often enhanced as they see with their physical eyes. We've been taught that a picture is worth a thousand words. Visuals communicate in ways that words alone cannot. You don't even need a wall. Just toss it on the floor!

What kinds of visual aids do you use when you teach? Kids' teachers have pictures, puzzles, books, blocks, home living toys, music, nature objects, and musical instruments. A cut-up picture doubles as a puzzle.

With older kids, teenagers, and adults, it is not uncommon to see teachers using posters, maps, butcher paper, video clips, PowerPoint presentations, tablets and computers to communicate visually with their group. Then there is the old standard, the whiteboard. If you could locate a classic book or two by LeRoy Ford, you'd learn a few tricks for using even basic "visual aids" like a chalkboard more creatively.[17]

Jesus, the Master Teacher, used plenty of visual aids as He taught. A boy with some loaves and fishes helped Jesus demonstrate His power. A cursed fig tree became an object lesson. Pointing out the temple as He sat teaching on the Mount of Olives, Jesus predicted its destruction. A coin in a fish's mouth revealed His knowledge of all things. A little child was beckoned by Jesus to show the disciples the simple faith it takes to enter His kingdom. He pointed to a field white for harvest to instruct His disciples to pray for more workers. He even wrote in the dirt. We could go on, but you get the idea. Jesus used visuals all the time. Shouldn't we?

Responding to a question as if it is an interruption will shut down listening.

The default teaching method of many teachers is lecture. When teaching turns into a presentation, conversation is lost. Some teachers can spend an entire Bible study hour on just one or two verses, parsing words and mining minutia. They worked hard on their presentation, and asking questions interrupts the presentation's flow. "Save your questions to the end" really means "I will cover everything so brilliantly, there will be no need for questions." There won't be any time, either. Don't be that guy. Unless you want people to stop listening—and maybe even stop attending.

As a general rule, guests should not be called on to say or read anything.

One more important aside before we move on. What are you going to ask guests to say? Generally speaking, nothing! Public speaking has usually been at the top of the lists of people's fears. Don't force people to speak publicly when they are not ready. Calling on guests to read Scripture is a double-no-no. In fact, we would encourage you not to randomly call on members to read, either. Volunteers are fine. Or you can write the "address" of the verses you want read on three or so index cards and ask members ahead of time to mark their place and be prepared to read. You may even choose people because of the translation they use. When you read, occasionally model what to do when you come across a difficult pronunciation by substituting "hard word" as you read!

You know that you are on your way to becoming a more balanced teacher when you realize that the members of your group should talk at least as much as you do. It's important for you to get the group talking. In order to do that, you've got to ask some great questions. So after you have decided what to say (and not say), it's time to consider "What am I going to ask?"

Chapter 3
Ask

We promote thinking more by the questions we ask than the answers we give.
–Rick Yount[18]

One of the most effective ways to help members engage in group Bible study is to ask compelling questions.

Sometimes the best answer to a question is another question.

Jesus asked questions when He taught. Sometimes He used questions to expose the hypocrisy of the religious leaders. Other times He asked questions to help people clarify their thinking. Scripture records many times when Jesus asked questions:

- *Just then, an expert in the law stood up to test Him, saying, "Teacher, what must I do to inherit eternal life?" "What is written in the law?" He asked him. "How do you read it?" (Luke 10:25-26)*

- *On the third day, they found [12-year old Jesus] in the temple complex sitting among the teachers, listening to them and asking them questions. (Luke 2:46)*

- *"Who do you say I am?" (Matt. 16:13-15)*

Sometimes the best thing to say is nothing.

Silence is golden. Most group leaders use questions in their groups, but most commit a teaching "sin" when they ask their questions: The teacher answers his or her own question when the group members don't answer right away. By doing this, a group leader inadvertently trains group members to wait for him to answer. The group leader wonders why people don't respond to his questions. The people have been trained to wait. Experience has taught them that the teacher is so uncomfortable with the silence, he'll answer his own question if they just wait him out.

Research indicates that the quality of the responses improves if the wait time after a teacher's question extends beyond three seconds to twenty seconds.[19] Group members—especially reflective learners—need time to process questions. Give it to them. In fact, sometimes let the group know you are going to wait twenty seconds for everybody to think.

If you want conversational community, you'll be silent a second or third time.

When twenty seconds of silence is finally broken, some teachers are so relieved they couldn't bear to do it again. But if you restrain yourself, smile at the first respondent and remain silent, someone else will respond. And if you can make yourself do it a third time, conversation will break out!

If you want to see how the conversation is going in your group, chart it.

Ask someone—maybe the person who talks too much—to chart the discussion for one or more sessions. Just print first names (or just an X) to represent each person and the approximate room set up (circle, semi-circle, rows, etc.). Every time there is a discussion question or other conversation starter, draw an arrow from the speaker to the person addressed.

Even teachers who pride themselves on discussion may discover something sobering. They are typically engaged in a series of dialogues rather than facilitating a conversation. That is, an arrow goes from a member to the teacher, and the teacher back to the member. Then from another member to the teacher, and back to the member. And so forth. With the effective use of silence, the chart will reveal more and more arrows between the members themselves, not just back and forth with the teacher. That's conversational community!

If you can't quit lecturing cold turkey, put a chair beside the lectern.

It is very difficult to facilitate a conversation when you are the only one standing. Teachers sometimes tell us, "My class just won't respond."

Try sitting down. Place a chair beside the lectern. Ask a well-crafted, relevant question. Then sit down. Be quiet. Wait. When you've had as much as you can take, stand!

This little drama emphasizes that you are serious about creating conversational community. Yes, some will freak out a little. But not nearly as much as the day they walk in the room and see it set up in a semi-circle. By the way, you can get about the same number of chairs in a semi-circle using three walls of a room as you can get in rows. If you create a circle using all four walls, you'll usually get more. Don't believe it's true? Just try it. We dare you. But beware. Conversational community could break out!

You may not have to ask a kid a question to get a conversation going.

Just sit down. On eye level. They will talk. Just be in a posture to listen. Ask clarifying questions. "What happened then?" "What emotions were expressed?" "What did you do next?" Make connections to the lesson as appropriate. But mostly just listen! It works with adults too.

Not all questions are created equal.

There is a real art and science to crafting great discussion questions. Discussion questions are exactly that: questions that generate discussion. But sometimes teachers mistake a question-and-answer (Q&A) question for a discussion question. What's the difference? Thank you for asking! A Q&A question asked in a group Bible study might be, "According to John 3:16, what did God do to prove His love for us?" (Answer: He sent His Son, Jesus, to die for us.) Nothing wrong, necessarily, with that question. It's a text-based question, but it's not a great discussion question. Here is how that question could be restated as a compelling discussion question: "What is the greatest act of love someone has done for you?" This question is open-ended and allows the one answering it to recall a situation and tell a story from their life. The question is emotive. It will very likely prompt others in the group to share their stories. See the difference? Now we've got a discussion question! And maybe a glimpse into conversational community.

Great questions are crafted. Questions made up on the spot are usually crummy.

One of the worst mistakes teachers make is to create questions on the spot. That almost always leads to disaster! Richards and Bredfeldt say:

Good questions do not just happen. One of the common mistakes teachers make is to think that they will be able to compose questions on the fly.[20]

Questions need contemplation. Questions need forethought. Teachers should avoid spontaneous questions in favor of those that are planned out. Words matter. Improve the quality of your teaching by improving the quality of the questions you ask. Great questions take time to craft.

Here are a few indicators that you have created a provocative discussion question set:

- *It moves your learners from general implications to specific personal application.*

- *It creates further dialogue and involves the group members.*

- *It is open-ended, rather than having a one-word answer.*

- *It invites everyone to talk and answer.*

There are a few places you'll find great questions. First, look in your Leader Guide. That tool is carefully crafted by Bible study experts who are skilled in thinking through a group experience, providing discussion questions that get people talking.

The *Serendipity Bible for Groups*[21] is also a wonderful resource. The questions are often thought-provoking and relevant. They just work. Sometimes a great question like the ones in the *Serendipity Bible* will cause you to think of another great question.

Different questions have different functions.

Teachers who are savvy realize that questions have different functions. Yount explains that some questions focus on recall of basic information, or knowledge. Other questions relate to understanding, moving the learner to a different level of learning. He classifies these understanding questions in the following way:

- **Comprehension questions.** *Calls for learners to interpret, compare, and explain a single concept. Questions include words such as describe, illustrate, and rephrase.*

- **Application questions.** *Learners take the next step by using the concept to solve a problem. Solve, classify, choose, and employ are words used in these questions.*

- **Analysis questions.** *Learners must identify causes and motives. Complex subjects must be broken down. Words such as analyze, conclude, infer, distinguish, and outline reflect this level.*

- **Synthesis questions.** *Require a group member to create a new complex concept, principle, or definition. Words like predict, construct, originate, design, and plan reflect this level.*

- **Evaluation questions.** *Call for people to judge or appraise the work of others—most often the result of synthesis. Words such as judge, argue, decide, and critique reflect this level.*

Yount also describes some questions you should think twice about using:
- **Simplistic questions.** *The answers are painfully obvious, and group members sometimes hesitate to answer these questions because they almost feel like trick questions.*

- **Leading questions.** *When a teacher asks this type of question, he or she is trying to elicit a particular answer from group members.*

- **Rhetorical questions.** *These are questions the group leader answers for the group. Yount's general rule of thumb is to never ask rhetorical questions of the group. Never ever.*[22]

There are a few standard questions.

- *[Name], do you have a view on this?*

- *How does that connect with what [name] just said?*

- *That's interesting. Can you think of biblical support for that?*

- *Would anyone who has not spoken like to add something?*

Conversational community can only happen if everyone in the group gets to talk.

What do you say to the person who says too much? That is probably the most frequently asked questions we get in training conferences. So let's deal with it right away. If you lead a Bible study group, odds are you've got a Talker. They can dominate a group conversation, often hijacking discussions away from other group members. They love to be the first person to answer a question, grind a personal axe, or advance a favorite theological conviction. If you are going to grow in your ability to lead and manage your group, you're going to have to deal with them at some point, and sooner is better than later.

Here are four ways:

1. **Call on specific people to answer questions.** If you have a Talker in your group, quickly shift your teaching strategy. Begin asking a specific person to answer a question. "Bill, how do you respond to question two?" sends a signal to your Talker that you value other people's input.

2. **Enlist the Talker to answer specific questions prior to the Bible study session.** If you have a Talker, it could make good sense to pre-enlist him to answer certain questions. This can serve to restrict his talking to two questions, giving other members of the group the opportunity to answer the remaining ones.

3. **Interrupt the Talker.** If your Talker just won't let go of the reins, you may have to interrupt him. Say something like, "Thanks for sharing your thoughts with us. I'm sorry to interrupt you, but I'd love to hear how Phil might respond to the question."

4. **Invite the Talker for some "coffee and confrontation."** Confronting the Talker can be intimidating. But at times it is necessary. Pray. Be honest. Thank the Talker for his contributions. Note that they sometimes keep others from fully participating. Reveal your plan to assign specific questions to others in the group to jumpstart conversation. Consider asking the Talker to be the designated listener. The job is to summarize the discussion when called upon; they may only speak to ask clarifying questions. By the way, this is also a great assignment for an apprentice teacher.[23]

Being included is better than being chosen.

Mark Jones, who directs the ministry to kids at Quail Springs Church in greater Oklahoma City, tells about being the last kid chosen for pick-up basketball games in his neighborhood. He got "picked" but not included. That's a challenge when teaching by discussion. The more experience you gain and the more you get to know your group members, the more you'll be able to help everyone be included. Community is about inclusion, not just membership. Ideally, members will invite each other into the conversation. That would be called conversational community!

Can you ask too many questions?

How many questions should you ask? If your Bible study group meets on Sunday mornings adjacent to your church's worship service, chances are you've got just 60-75 minutes to meet as a group. The actual Bible study portion of that time tends to be about 30-45 minutes, depending on the church's schedule. That's not a lot of time! How many discussion questions should a teacher be prepared to ask?

We believe that five well-crafted discussion questions are about right. Some of you are protesting. "That's crazy! Five questions? That's not nearly enough!" We thought the same thing before we re-launched the *Bible Studies For Life* series. Five is enough. For three years, I (Ken) have used it every Sunday. All I've planned on asking are the five discussion questions from the Leader Guide. And maybe one extra "just in case." I rarely need the extra one.

My group has about 40-45 minutes for Bible study. If I ask five great discussion questions, and if they take five minutes each to discuss (normally it takes longer), then 25 of my 45 minutes is consumed. If I spend just five minutes opening the lesson and another five minutes ending it and helping my group discover how to apply it, my time is almost completely gone! By the time I say a few things that are relevant about the text for understanding, we've studied the Bible for a solid 45 minutes.

Choosing the right questions starts with anticipating the questions they may ask you.

As you study and prepare your lesson, a good habit is to ask yourself, "What questions might my group members have for me about this passage?" Learn to prepare with that in mind, and you'll have questions that connect with the group. It will make your leadership of the group more effective, and you'll gain the respect of your people when you say to them, "That's a great question! I wondered the same thing this week, so I studied more on that subject, and here's what I discovered…"

If you reward preparation, you'll get more and better questions.

One way to reward members for preparing for the group is to start the session with some questions:

- *Did anyone circle something puzzling in your Personal Study Guide (PSG) you want to know more about?*

- *Did anyone mark something a writer said that you'd like clarified?*

- *Did anyone highlight a particularly meaningful sentence?*

What other questions might you add? Teachers who reward preparation will also encourage questions. And teachers who encourage questions will have to work harder! The group members will come into the group time knowing stuff. That's great!

"I don't know" always beats making stuff up.

What if you don't know the answer? You don't have to have all the answers! In fact, you probably can't have all the answers to the questions your members will ask. It's humanly impossible! An honest, "I don't know the answer to your question, but I will find one" is all you need to say in response. Don't be a know-it-all. They always get exposed sooner or later! Teachers are simply "learners among learners." It's OK to admit that you're still being taught new things by the Lord. Your honesty will be rewarded with the respect of your group members.

Never single out a guest to answer a question.

What should you ask a guest during the group time? Generally speaking, nothing directly! Instead, include indirect questions addressed to the entire group. Leave it up to the guest. One idea you may want to use to make sure guests don't feel singled out is using index cards. Pass out index cards and ask the group members and guests to write a question they have about the passage being studied, and turn them in to you without signing their name. Rifle through the questions and pick out the best ones to answer. Who knows? One may belong to a guest! You can also have your group members text or email you their questions in advance of the Bible study so you have time to find answers.

There are better questions than "Did you have fun?"

It's OK to ask a child, "Did you have fun in your class today?" But by all means, don't stop there, parents! You are the spiritual leaders and teachers of your children (Deut. 6:6-9). The church is there to help you in that responsibility. Continuing a dialogue outside of your child's class is important to their spiritual growth. What would you add to this list of questions for kids?

- *What did you learn today?*
- *Who were some of the characters in the Bible story?*
- *What does Jesus want to help you do differently this week?*
- *Would you recite your memory verse for me?*
- *What was the most important thing you learned today?*
- *How can I pray for you?*

To help parents create conversations with their kids, LifeWay provides resources like family cards, Take-Home Activity Pages, and free apps. These simple tools create simple conversations to make certain that little minds are grasping simple but profoundly important truths.

Kids are more likely than adults to answer "What did you DO today?"

Adult and student teachers are going to Say certain things based upon their study and the needs of their group. Teachers will also Ask questions to help group members dig into God's Word and find meaning and application points. Next, we will consider an often neglected part of adult Bible study: what our group members Do. Kids' classes have it on adults here. Do is foundational for them! Adult groups could learn a thing or two about conversational community by observing a group of kids.

Adult teachers could learn some things from preschool teachers.

Our friend Dwayne McCrary wrote a great article about this for LifeWay's Groups blog (*LifeWay.com/GroupMinistry*). An expert adult teacher, he was asked to lead "group time" in a preschool class. Here are nine lessons he learned:

1. What they can see matters. Nothing gets by a 4-year old and that includes what is on the walls, even if you did not put it there. The first Sunday I was with the group, one child noticed a poster on the wall that had nothing to do with our study. Nevertheless, I spent all my time dealing with a distraction.

2. Class starts the moment the first child arrives. You can't tell 4-year olds to sit down and wait for everyone else to arrive. The class starts when the first one arrives and isn't over until the last one leaves.

3. Names are important. We have name tags that work as security as well. The first names are printed larger so they can be easily read, but the name tag usually gets attached on the child's back. The children expected me to know their names and to pronounce them correctly.

4. Flexibility is a must. We have a plan but something always happens. Storms in the area, an overflowing toilet, or an art project that takes longer than expected (or worse, takes less time than expected) all force you to be flexible.

5. What you think is a goofy idea usually is the one that works best. The idea was to make a donkey out of a paper bag and then to color a paper cover to go on the back of the donkey. I thought this was a doomed idea, but I was wrong. The children colored both sides of the cover, making different designs on each side. They explained to their parents what their design symbolized and why their cover would have been perfect for Jesus to sit on as He rode into Jerusalem.

6. It is about the Bible. Even 4-year olds expect us to read the Bible and to talk about it. We may do all kinds of things, but if we don't reference the Bible or a Bible story, they let us know about it.

7. They want to participate in the process. One child was having trouble removing stickers from a sheet, so I thought I would step in. I was clearly informed by that struggling child that my help was not needed. The tone used was not sassy or mean. She simply wanted to participate in the experience, even if it took a while to get finished.

8. Routines give a framework. We followed the same pattern every week, and I thought it would be good to shake things up after a few weeks. The group knew our pattern and let us know we were not following it. The pattern was important to them, giving the group a sense of security. Changing it just to change it only confused and frustrated the group.

9. If you let them talk, they will. There have been many times when kids have talked about some serious things while playing in a kitchen or building a block wall. I needed to listen and let them talk. I learned more than they did.

Dwayne concluded: "I am sure there are others lessons I am learning; I just don't know it yet. These same lessons are true when teaching adults. The group time starts when the first person arrives. Adults expect me to know their names. Adults want to participate in the group time. I'm a better teacher of adults as a result of teaching 4-year olds!"

Chapter 4
Do

PowerPoint® isn't required to make a powerful point.

Jesus is known as the Master Teacher. He taught in a day when there were no dry-erase markers, tablets, or data projectors. There was no formal curriculum or teaching plan for Him to follow. No Leader Pack full of maps, posters, and other helps. Yet, He was Master Teacher. His arsenal of methods was limitless. He always used just the right method for the environment, the size of the group, and the maturity of the learners.

When the Agent of creation taught, He creatively used a lot of methods.

Robert Joseph Choun chronicled 20 examples of Jesus' use of varied methodology. How many of the following have you used with your group in the past month? quarter? year?

- *Object lessons (John 4:1-42)*
- *Points of contact (John 1:35-51)*
- *Aims (John 4:34)*
- *Problem-solving (Mark 10:17-22)*
- *Conversation (Mark 10:27)*
- *Questions (As recorded in the Gospels, Jesus asked over 100 questions to provoke people to think and seek the truth.)*
- *Answers (Jesus used His answers to move people from where they were to where they needed to be in order to grow spiritually. Jesus encouraged people to discover the truth.)*
- *Lecture (Matt. 5–7; John 14–17)*
- *Parables (John 10:1-21; 15:1-10)*
- *Scripture (Jesus quoted extensively from the Old Testament when teaching.)*

- *Teachable moments (John 4:5-26)*
- *Contrast (Matt. 5:21-22,33-34,38-39)*
- *Concrete and literal examples (Matt. 6:26-34)*
- *Symbols (Matt. 26:17-20)*
- *Large and small groups (Matt. 5–7; John 14–17)*
- *Individual teaching opportunities (John 3:1-21)*
- *Modeling (Matt. 15:32)*
- *Motivation (Matt. 16:24-27)*
- *Impression and expression (Matt. 4:19-20; 7:20)*
- *Himself (Matt. 28:19-20)* [24]

It should be pretty apparent that Jesus epitomized creativity in teaching. He said things, asked things, and led people to do things. This should be our goal as well.

When the One who designed the brain communicates, He does more than talk to it.

How does God communicate? Hebrews 1:1-2 provides insight: *Long ago God spoke to the fathers by the prophets* **at different times and in different ways.** *In these last days, He has spoken to us by His Son* (HCSB, emphasis added). Other translations of Scripture add shades of meaning:
- *Many times and in many ways… (ESV)*
- *At various times and in various ways… (NKJV)*
- *Many times and in various ways… (NIV)*
- *At sundry times and in divers manners… (KJV)*

One thing is for sure: God communicated regularly and with variety. You can deliver content to your group in a classroom, living room, or other meeting place using a variety of ways, too. There are several approaches to learning, and every group has people that prefer to learn differently. If you practice using multiple approaches, you'll find yourself meeting the needs of more group members more often.

Learners like activity when they experience it, but they'll vote for passivity if you ask. Don't.

Some adult group members are hoping to do nothing but "sit and soak." Their idea of a perfect class is to come and listen to a well-prepared teacher. They are content with learning a new fact, a new piece of information, or a new insight into Scripture they've never heard before.

But others are hoping to do things. They long for blanks to fill in, a case study to exam, a position to debate, a chart to complete, a quiz to take, or an object to hold. This would be me (Ken). Although I like an interesting lecture, I find that my mind wanders. Does yours? I prefer a group that provides me with active learning options. I prefer that those options be varied and mixed up a little, leaving me guessing as to which ones will be used in the group today. That, I believe, is the majority of us.

Guests can participate in the conversation if we provide the help they need.

Guests can be included by providing them with the tools to be involved. A Personal Study Guide is a great start. Giving them their own copy serves as an invitation to participate and a means for them to figure out what is going on. This tool also makes it possible for the guest to more readily participate since they have access to the same information as everyone else. We believe in using every tool available to help every person who attends our group to participate in Bible study.

Transformational discipleship seldom results from a passive approach to learning—or a presentation approach to teaching.

In the book *Transformational Discipleship*, the authors report a key insight related to active and passive learning. They conclude that one-way communication from teacher to student is not a healthy philosophy.

If we settle for only dispensing information, not only will change in people's lives fall short of transformation, but we will begin to lead people down a dangerous path...people will begin to define their discipleship exclusively in terms of intellect. That is, if you know the right answers, you are following Jesus more and more closely.[25]

There is nothing wrong with lecturing on occasion; you just don't want to have a steady diet of it. It would be like taking your family to a restaurant that offers a great buffet, but only allowing them to fill up their plates with a single item. Actually, lecture is more like having your family sit and watch you eat off the buffet, then describing how the food tasted.

The introduction and conclusion are the best time to mix it up and break the normal routine.

If you are stuck in a method "rut" in your group, a great place to try out new ways of teaching is during the introduction of the group session. You'll use this time to stimulate interest and spark a desire to discover what the Bible says. A second natural place to try a new teaching method is at the end of the Bible study, as you draw conclusions and lead the group to do something in response to what they have discovered in God's Word.

A great teaching plan is set apart from a good one by what gets said and asked–and what does not.

This is at least as important as deciding what you will Say, Ask, and Do. An important related question is what part of the Scripture passage might not be covered in detail? Based on the time available, the needs of the group, the lesson, and other factors, you may need to do nothing more than read some of the verses in the chosen passage. In a class for kids, you do not have to do all the suggested activities. Yes, it is okay to skip some! More content almost never results in more learning. In fact, less content thoroughly explored and applied almost always results in greater learning.

The key to a great teaching plan is to have a clear aim for every group session.

What's the big idea? The main thought? The preferred outcome? The 3 A.M. Statement? If you can get that crystal clear in your mind going into a group time, it will help you focus. It will help you avoid distractions.

It will help you re-focus the group. It will help you decide what not to Say, Ask, and Do. So that you can get to the big question: "What do we do with this?" That is, what is the call to obedience? Why should we obey?

Effective teaching is transformactional. It's about leading the group to DO something.

Jesus gave the gift of shepherd-teacher to His church (Eph. 4:11ff). Their purpose: to equip the saints (every member of His Body) to stand, serve, and share. Obedience is what we are leading the group to Do.

Coining a new word, Rick and Shera Melick argue that great teaching should be "transformactional." Real transformation is demonstrated by action.[26] We must move them beyond simply believing or accepting a truth. Transformation requires obedience to that truth. Don't be tempted to accept the idea that your only responsibility is to present the truth. Certainly we help them discover the truth, but that is only half of the job. As teachers, we have the responsibility of challenging them to act on that truth.

Disciples are marked by obedience to what they know, not just by what they know.

This is particularly important in our day when information is so abundant. We live in a time of affluence when the largest challenge to our faith is not persecution but instead materialism–the opposite prong on the same pitchfork. Our playlists abound with countless sermons and unbridled access to biblical teaching. Most of us live within a stone's throw of not one, not two, but at least three faithful, evangelical churches. The number of books by dead theologians is beyond what we can consume. At any given moment, we can be reading, listening to, or even watching centuries of commentary, study, and reflection on any biblical text we so choose.

If you'll excuse the metaphor, we are at risk of being intellectually fat Christians, minds obese with knowledge and bloated with facts.

Too much knowledge can make you over-educated and under-obedient.

You know it is happening to you when you tend to have **an attitude of examination rather than participation.** Like a food critic who can't really enjoy the meal. If you find yourself surrounded by the teaching of the Word and the fellowship of the saints, but critically examining the methodology of those leading rather than participating in what's going on around you, it's very possible that you have begun to be overtaken by your education. In a case like that, you would prefer to analyze the details of the presentation rather than dwelling on the content and the presence of God.

A second stage of over-education is when **you are more excited than grieved at finding the fault.** Like a spiritual food critic. If during that examination you do indeed find fault, and maybe it's something relatively minor, do you feel a sense of justification? We know that feeling, too. It's a sense of triumph that somehow you have been able to mine through all the external fluff and find that kernel of error that simply must be exposed. And if it's not exposed to the world, at least it's exposed to your own heart. When we feel that, we are feeding that animal of superiority that lurks in us all, that beast which craves a higher place over all others so that we might not feel so small, even for a moment.

You know for sure you're over-educated and under-obedienced when **you desire generalities over personal specifics.** If, when you find yourself in a conversation where there is no confession of sin, no admittance of struggle, and no grace to listen to another do the same, but rather hypothetical "can God make a rock so big He couldn't move it?" kinds of discussions, then beware of over-education. In a case like this, we keep the truth of God and the conviction of the Holy Spirit at arm's length because we fear what might happen to us if it, and He, came any closer. Surely something would have to change, and we can't bear the thought of the magnifying glass of our gaze being turned inward. It should not be so. For individuals or for groups. It affects both.

The real test of conversational community is not the pursuit of lofty thoughts or intimate fellowship, but the pursuit of obedience.

But be doers of the word and not hearers only. (James 1:22)

Community is not meant to be a group counseling session; it's not merely an opportunity for open and honest discussion. The end of biblical community, as the writer of Hebrews put it, is meant to move us toward greater holiness:

> *And let us be concerned about one another in order to promote love and good works, not staying away from our worship meetings, as some habitually do, but encouraging each other, and all the more as you see the day drawing near (Heb. 10:24-25).*

We must not stop at merely sharing with each other; we must move further into helping each other obey. The teacher can't find the "win" by asking whether or not people talked, whether the discussion was lively, or whether it was truly transparent. We must move people to specific action points of obedience. Allan Taylor gets straight to heart of the matter:

> *Teachers should teach for the sake of obedience and not just for the sake of knowledge. Imparting knowledge is certainly needed because people cannot be obedient to that of which they are ignorant. We must teach to impart knowledge, but we must not stop there. Teachers have got to see this truth with a sharp focus. Leading people to obey must be the focus of every lesson.*[27]

In conversational community, obey and walk and hear and talk pretty much mean the same thing.

Biblically speaking, two pairs of words are so close in meaning that any difference is barely distinguishable:

- **Hear** *and* **obey**
- **Talk** *and* **walk**

Hear and obey, for there's no other way. "Hear, O Israel" was not a call to "Listen up." It was a call to obey. Not to obey is not to have really heard.

The Great Commission is the church's marching order, given by the Lord Himself. In those verses, we discover that we are to make disciples, teaching them to obey everything the Lord commanded. The emphasis is on obey; not on "everything." The goal of our teaching isn't classrooms packed with people who are full of biblical knowledge (although knowing what the Bible says is very important). The goal is to teach men, women, boys, and girls in such a way that they understand, respond to, and obey Jesus.

We don't want a room full of people who obey out of fear or because they believe it makes them more acceptable to God. We want people to fall in love with the One who loved them enough to leave heaven, empty Himself, and die in their place. We want people who are radically in love with Jesus, not just rule-following Christians who measure their holiness by the number of commands they keep—or think they keep.

"Conversation" now refers to "talk." It used to refer to "walk."

I (David) love the way "conversation" is used in the King James Version. But words have a way of changing their meaning over time. Not too many years after it was published in 1611, the meaning of the word "conversation" started shifting from "walk" to "talk." Note how the Greek word *anastrophe* was translated then versus now:

- *Ephesians 4:22:*

   That ye put off concerning the **former conversation** *the old man, which is corrupt according to the deceitful lusts. (KJV)*

   You took off your **former way of life**, *the old self that is corrupted by deceitful desires. (HCSB)*

- *Philippians 1:27:*

  Only let your **conversation** *be as it becometh the gospel of Christ.*
  (KJV)

  Just one thing: Live your **life** *in a manner worthy of the gospel of*
  Christ. (HCSB)

- *1 Peter 1:15 ;*

  But as he which hath called you is holy, so be ye holy in **all manner**
  of conversation. *(KJV)*

  But as the One who called you is holy, you also are to be holy in **all your**
  conduct. *(HCSB)*

- *James 3:13*

  Who is a wise man and endued with knowledge among you? let him
  shew out of a **good conversation** *his works with meekness of wisdom.*
  (KJV)

  Who is wise and has understanding among you? He should show his
  works by **good conduct** *with wisdom's gentleness. (HCSB)*

So, although the use of "conversation" is now used to refer to our talk,
it used to refer to our walk. Shouldn't they be the same anyway? So
"conversational community" is about obedience in talk and walk. They go
together. And together they go.

The call to obedience is often plural.

If Bibles employed the word "y'all" to distinguish between "you" singular
and "you" plural, it would use the abbreviation for "you all" a lot.
Obedience is not just something individuals do as a result of conversational
community. It is something communities do together. Dave Earley says it
well:

Life is not meant to be lived as only "Jesus and me."

It is meant to be lived as "Jesus and we."[28]

Obedience is its own answer to "why?"

Why obey? The gospel. In order to understand, we must know the difference between the indicatives and imperatives of the gospel. The solid unchanging truth that God took on flesh, came to earth, and satisfied His own justice through death on the cross in our place is the indicative truth of the gospel. But the indicatives don't stop there.

When we believe this truth, we actually become a "new creation" (2 Cor. 5:17). Our old, dead, hard-as-stone hearts are replaced with something brand new. We have become, because of Jesus, the righteousness of God, and now God freely calls us His sons and daughters. This, too, is an indicative truth of the gospel.

But these indicatives also carry with them imperatives. In other words, because we have become something new, our behavior or our walk must follow what we have become.

This is Paul's pattern in his epistles. Look closely and you'll see that he almost always began with the indicatives of the gospel. He told us the truth about the pervasive nature of sin and our need for a Savior. Then he reminded us of what we've become in Christ. It's not until he has reminded us of these indicatives that he comes to our behavior. Imperatives result in indicatives. We behave because we have become.

When we align our outward behavior with the expressed will of God in His Word, we are behaving in accordance with what we have already become. As we grow in Christ and our behavior falls more and more in line with His heart, we are living out the dramatic and irreversible change that the gospel has wrought inside of us.

Sometimes, then, we try and complicate the issue too much. We look at the clouds and wonder what God's will is for our lives, when more times than not, God's will is perfectly plain. And that will is most commonly expressed and lived out in the context of our relationships with others.

The call to obedience is often obvious.

Read through the Bible looking for commands and you will discover obedience has a place in Christianity. We don't obey to gain our salvation, but because of it. So what are we called on to do?

The one anothers. Some negative: *Don't lie to. Don't judge. Don't grumble. Don't bite!* Mostly positive: *Greet. Encourage. Accept. Forgive. Spur on. Confess to. Pray for. Comfort. Show hospitality to. Regard. Serve. Tolerate. Love.*

The general don'ts: *Murder. Lie. Steal. Covet. Cheat. Forsake assembling. Be proud.*
The general dos: *Be strong. Have courage. Seek wisdom. Abide. Honor. Submit. Wait. Watch. Go. Teach. Obey. Rejoice. Always. Rejoice. And again.*

Be: *Blameless. Holy. Glad. Wise. Alert. Shrewd. Strong. Glad. Content. Thankful. Generous. Quick to hear. Slow to speak. Slow to anger. Still.*
Be: *Fruitful. Love. Joy. Peace. Patience. Kindness. Goodness. Gentleness. Self-control. Faith.* Add: *Knowledge. Endurance. Godliness. Brotherly affection.*
Be: *Conformed to His image.*

Don't be: *Conformed to the world.*
But: *Transformed. Fervent. Patient. Persistent. Steadfast. Immovable.*

Ask. *Knock.* Seek: *Justice.* Show: *Mercy.* Walk: *Humbly.*

Love: *Bear. Believe. Hope. Endure. Patient. Kind.*
Is Not: *Envious. Boastful. Conceited. Selfish. Provoked.*

Pursue: *Righteousness. Godliness. Faith. Love. Endurance.*
Dwell: *On whatever is True. Honorable. Just. Pure. Lovely. Commendable.*
Love: *The Lord. Heart. Mind. Strength. Neighbor. Self.*

Don't be: *Ashamed. Arrogant. Afraid. Lots of times. Don't be afraid. Over and again. Fear not.*

Be: *Light. Salt.*

Conversational community provides salt.

Every time a group or class gathers, members should be equipped to obey the Great Commission. Every member should leave the group with some "salt" he or she can sprinkle into conversations. Salt sprinkled with love naturally and winsomely in the course of everyday conversations. As they go. That is the sense of the Great Commission. "As you go" along life's way, the Truth, the Life, and the Way will provide natural, unforced, divinely-appointed opportunities for conversations. About Him.

Obedience is never just about what and how and why we obey; it is always about Who.

In conversational community, our pursuit of obedience is not about pacifying or persuading some distant oligarch. It is about pleasing the self-revealing "I Am." Learning of and from Him is an act of obedience. He desires for us to know Him. In community, we can know him biblically and experientially.

Throughout history, God has commanded His people to remember. The festivals in the Old Testament and the Lord's Supper in the New Testament were given to the people of God so that they might remember. This is God's grace to us because we are a forgetful people. We are those who tend to lapse into a state of spiritual sleepwalking, going through the motions of our lives, while all those things which are most important fade into the background. This remembering is accomplished by more than keeping dates on the calendar. It's accomplished through the people of God when they relate rightly to each other.

When we forgive each other freely and quickly, we are reminded He is the great Forgiver. When we call each other to obedience, we are reminded of the Holy Creator. When we tell the truth to one another, we are reminded of the greatest Truth. When we immerse ourselves in each other's lives, even in the most uncomfortable situations, we are reminded of the God who took on flesh and immersed Himself in our world.

We remind each other of the Father, the Provider, the Pursuer, the Bread, the Living Water… and the Teacher.

"Teacher"

When your earthly life is celebrated at your memorial service, few memories will surpass those of the people who remember you as "teacher."

The members and groups you impact as a teacher may never know anything about the concepts in this book. Teaching aims. 3 A.M.s. Conversational community. Four voices. Transformational Sweet Spot. Say/Ask/Do. Cutting floor paradox. Premastication!

They may never say the words "conversational community." They don't need to. They just need to experience it. When they do, they may call you a name. You'd be blessed if the name they call you is "teacher."

Someday, folks will gather to remember your life. There are not many better things people could say about you on that day other than about your calling to teach the Bible. "She taught kids in Sunday School as long as she had strength." "He taught middle school boys the Bible for 50 years." "She was the best Bible teacher I ever had." "He was a teacher who was always learning." "She knew God's Story so well; she knew our stories well, too."

Thank you for answering the call to teach. May your ministry be marked by an unquenchable devotion to the Word. And an insatiable desire to create environments and experiences that help boys and girls and men and women engage and embrace the Word in conversational community.

It is told of a young boy's testimony: "First, I fell in love with my teacher. Then I fell in love with my teacher's Bible. Then I fell in love with my teacher's Lord."

You'll rarely cover everything you want to.
You'll just run out of time. Or pages.

Appendix
Creating a Development Plan

As teachers of God's Word, we should be the first to line up for further development. A branch of our military uses the phrase "be all you can be" to inspire young people to commit to years of service. Those new recruits are challenged to lay aside personal comforts. They are asked to sacrifice. They are challenged to develop. Isn't it time for you and I to respond to a similar challenge? Should we not "be all we can be" for the sake of the King and His kingdom? Shouldn't we seek to develop ourselves into more effective kingdom leaders?

The list that follows represents subject matter categories to be included in a development plan for a teacher-shepherd-leader. Don't let these things overwhelm you. Start small. Start slowly. Just start. Take the initiative. Be all you can be. Take responsibility for developing yourself. As you grow, help others develop themselves, too. Take someone with you on this journey.

The purpose of this list is to identify areas of competency. A variety of resources could be used to sharpen your understanding or skill. New resources are being produced regularly. Make sure you stay fresh and up to date by utilizing new resources in each category and continuing to grow stronger in each area.

General

- *Sharing Jesus*
- *Group ministry purpose and vision*
- *Organizing a group*
- *Enlisting others*
- *Caring ministry how-tos*
- *Contacting group members*
- *Crisis ministry*
- *Planning service projects*

- *Starting new groups*
- *Mentoring others*

Bible
- *Biblical backgrounds*

  Specifics about each Bible book
  Key biblical personalities
  Biblical history
  Biblical timelines
  Significant places in biblical history

- *Biblical doctrine*

  The Baptist Faith & Message
  Key doctrinal terms/concepts

- *Spiritual disciplines*
- *Personal Bible study skills*

Holy Spirit
- *Spiritual development*
- *Spiritual gifts*
- *Listening skills*
- *Fostering concern for others*

Learner
- *Educational philosophy / psychology*
- *Age group characteristics/generations/human development*

  LifeWay's "Levels of Biblical Learning" (preschool throuhg sixth
  grade)

- *Group dynamics*
- *Teaching principles*
- *How people learn*

Leader

- *Preparing to teach*
- *Creating a group plan*
- *Motivating the learner*
- *Teaching for transformation*
- *Delivering presentations*
- *Using visuals and media*
- *Leading discussion*
- *Crafting question sets*
- *Teaching methods*
- *Choosing curriculum*
- *Class management*
- *Change management*
- *Conflict management*
- *Team building*
- *Leadership styles*

Blogs and websites – free articles from trusted sources

- *KenBraddy.com*
- *GroupsMatter.com*
- *LifeWay.com/GroupMinistry*
- *SundaySchoolLeader.com*

Events to Consider Attending

LifeWay conducts various training events through the year that are designed just for leaders. You can find these by going to *LifeWay.com* and perusing through the list in the drop-down menu under "Events" on the top bar (visit the items listed under "Church Leadership" first).

Endnotes

1. See John 13:13.

2. Gary Newton, *Heart-Deep Teaching: Engaging Students for Transformed Lives* (Nashville: B&H Academic, 2012).

3. Eric Geiger, Philip Nation, and Michael Kelley, *Transformational Discipleship* (Nashville: B&H, 2012) 58-63.

4. Charles B. Williams, *The New Testament: A Translation in the Language of the People,* rev. ed. (Chicago: Moody Press, 1950).

5. Maurice Hodges, *Teaching to Change Lives* (C.1990. P.O. Box 482, Smackover, AR 71762).

6. The Baptist Faith and Message was adopted by the Southern Baptist Convention in 2000. Available online at *SBC.net.* The companion book can be ordered from *LifeWay.com.*

7. "Levels of Biblical Learning" (Nashville: LifeWay Press, 2009). A free PDF download is available at *LifeWay.com/LevelsOfBiblicalLearning.*

8. Howard Gardner, *Multiple Intelligences, revised* (New York: Basic Books, 2006).

9. Thomas Armstrong, *Seven Kinds of Smart, updated* (New York: Plume, 1999).

10. Brad Waggoner, *The Shape of Faith to Come* (Nashville: B&H, 2008) 273-286.

11. Email exchange between David Francis and Shelly Taylor. Edited.

12. Allan Taylor, *Sunday School in HD* (Nashville: B&H, 2009), 149-152.

13. William R. Yount, *Created to Learn: A Christian Teacher's Introduction to Educational Psychology* (Nashville: B&H Academic, 2010), 342-343.

14. Newton, 63-69.

15. Lawrence O. Richards and Richard Bredfeltd, *Creative Bible Teaching* (Chicago: Moody, 1998), 189-191.

16. For more detail, see David Francis, *Missionary Sunday School* (Nashville: LifeWay Press, 2011), 8-12.

17. Leroy Ford, *Tools for Teaching and Training* (Nashville: Broadman Press, 1961) and *A Primer for Teachers and Leaders* (Nashville: Broadman Press, 1963).

18. Yount, 353.

19. Robert Pazmino, *Basics of Teaching for Christians* (Grand Rapids: Baker Book House, 1998), 68.

20. Richards and Bredfeldt, 191.

21. Lyman Coleman, ed., *Serendipity Bible for Groups* (Littleton: Serendipity House, 1998).

22. Yount, 465-66.

23. For more ideas, see Stephen Brookfield and Stephen Preskill, *Discussion as a Way of Teaching* (San Francisco: Jossey-Bass, 2005) 169-177. For brief highlights from this book applied to Christian education, see *The Discover Triad* by David Francis (free download at *LifeWay.com/DavidFrancis*).

24. Kenneht O. Gangel and Howard G. Hendricks, ed., *The Christian Educator's Handbook on Teaching* (Grand Rapids: Baker Academics, 1998), 166-168.

25. Geiger, Nation, Kelley, 207.

26. Rick Melick and Shera Melick, *Teaching That Transforms: Facilitating Life Change Through Adult Bible Teaching* (Nashville: B&H Academic, 2010).

27. Taylor, 58.

28. Dave Earley and Rod Dempsey. *Disciple Making Is...* (Nashville: B&H Academic, 2013), 71.

Training helps utilizing this resource are avaialbe at *LifeWay.com/DavidFrancis* including the following: Conference Plans (for all leaders with adaptations for age group leaders), Presentation Support (backgrounds), Clipart (for promotion), and Conversation Points (ideas for discussing concepts in this book over coffee and other informal settings).

Notes and Reflections: